Yarasistan: My Wounds, My Crown

Abhijit Naskar is the 21st century Neuroscientist and Poet who has been serving at the forefront of humankind's struggle against inhumanity. As an untiring advocate of mental health and global harmony, he became a beloved best-selling author across the world with his very first book "The Art of Neuroscience in Everything". With his revolutionary contributions in Cognitive and Behavioral Neuroscience Naskar has helped the world tackle the horrors of systemic racism, biases, hate, extremism, discrimination and stereotypes more effectively, because of which he is lovingly hailed by humankind as 'the humanitarian scientist'.

Yarasistan

My Wounds,
My Crown

ABHIJIT
NASKAR

Also by Abhijit Naskar

The Art of Neuroscience in Everything
Your Own Neuron: A Tour of Your Psychic Brain
The God Parasite: Revelation of Neuroscience
The Spirituality Engine
Love Sutra: The Neuroscientific Manual of Love
Homo: A Brief History of Consciousness
Neurosutra: The Abhijit Naskar Collection
Autobiography of God: Biopsy of A Cognitive Reality
Biopsy of Religions: Neuroanalysis towards Universal
Tolerance
Prescription: Treating India's Soul
What is Mind?
In Search of Divinity: Journey to The Kingdom of Conscience
Love, God & Neurons: Memoir of a scientist who found
himself by getting lost
The Islamophobic Civilization: Voyage of Acceptance
Neurons of Jesus: Mind of A Teacher, Spouse & Thinker
Neurons, Oxygen & Nanak
The Education Decree
Principia Humanitas
The Krishna Cancer
Rowdy Buddha: The First Sapiens
We Are All Black: A Treatise on Racism
The Bengal Tigress: A Treatise on Gender Equality
Either Civilized or Phobic: A Treatise on Homosexuality
Wise Mating: A Treatise on Monogamy
Illusion of Religion: A Treatise on Religious
Fundamentalism
The Film Testament
Human Making is Our Mission: A Treatise on Parenting
I Am The Thread: My Mission
7 Billion Gods: Humans Above All
Lord is My Sheep: Gospel of Human
Morality Absolute
A Push in Perception
Let The Poor Be Your God
Conscience over Nonsense
Saint of The Sapiens
Time to Save Medicine
Fabric of Humanity
Build Bridges not Walls: In the name of Americana
The Constitution of The United Peoples of Earth

Lives to Serve Before I Sleep
When Humans Unite: Making A World Without Borders
All For Acceptance
Monk Meets World
Mission Reality
Citizens of Peace: Beyond The Savagery of Sovereignty
Operation Justice: To Make A Society That Needs No Law
See No Gender
The Gospel of Technology
Every Generation Needs Caretakers: The Gospel of
Patriotism
Aşkanjali: The Sufi Sermon
Mad About Humans: World Maker's Almanac
Revolution Indomable
When Call The People: My World My Responsibility
No Foreigner Only Family
Hurricane Humans: Give me accountability, I'll give you
peace
Ain't Enough to Look Human
Servitude is Sanctitude
Time To End Democracy: The Meritocratic Manifesto
I Vicdansaadet Speaking: No Rest Till The World is Lifted
Boldly Comes Justice: Sentient not Silent
Good Scientist: When Science and Service Combine
Sleepless for Society
Neden Türk: The Gospel of Secularism
Martyr Meets World: To Solve The Hard Problem of
Inhumanity
The Shape of A Human: Our America Their America
When Veins Ignite: Either Integration or Degradation
Heart Force One: Need No Gun to Defend Society
Solo Standing on Guard: Life Before Law
Generation Corazon: Nationalism is Terrorism
Mucize Insan: When The World is Family
Hometown Human: To Live For Soil and Society
Girl Over God: The Novel
Gente Mente Adelante: Prejudice Conquered is World
Conquered
Earthquakin' Egalitarian: I Die Everyday So Your Children
Can Live
Giants in Jeans: 100 Sonnets of United Earth
Vatican Virus: The Forbidden Fiction (Abi Naskar
Adventures Book 2)
Karadeniz Chronicle: The Novel (Abi Naskar Adventures

Book 3)
Şehit Sevda Society: Even in Death I Shall Live
Handcrafted Humanity: 100 Sonnets For A Blunderful
World
Mücadele Muhabbet: Gospel of An Unarmed Soldier
Making Britain Civilized: How to Gain Readmission to The
Human Race
Dervish Advaitam: Gospel of Sacred Feminines and Holy
Fathers
Honor He Wrote: 100 Sonnets For Humans Not Vegetables
The Gentalist: There's No Social Work, Only Family Work
Either Reformist or Terrorist: If You Are Terror I Am Your
Grandfather
Woman Over World: The Novel (Abi Naskar Adventures
Book 4)
High Voltage Habib: Gospel of Undoctrination
Bulldozer on Duty
Find A Cause Outside Yourself: Sermon of Sustainability
Ingan Impossible: Handbook of Hatebusting
Amor Apocalypse: Canım Sana İhtiyacım
Amantes Assemble: 100 Sonnets of Servant Sultans
Mucize Misafir Merhaba: The Peace Testament
Divane Dynamite: Only truth in the cosmos is love
Sin Dios Sí Hay Divinidad: The Pastor Who Never Was
Corazon Calamidad: Obedient to None, Oppressive to None
Esperanza Impossible: 100 Sonnets of Ethics, Engineering &
Existence
Mukemmel Musalman: Kafir Biraz, Peygamber Biraz
Himalayan Sonneteer: 100 Sonnets of Unsubmission

DEDICATION

To those who make others smile
overlooking their own sorrow.

CONTENTS

Part 1

Part 1

Let us leave,
let us leave all.
Let us leave the self,
as well as the fake world.

Let us leave behind all lies,
as well as all half-truth.
Let us leave ourselves as well,
so we could find life anew.

Let us forget what we are,
so we could wipe all divide away.
Let us leave behind all assumption,
so we could be each other's way.

Ben gidim, dostum,
benimle gelir misin?
Hadi gel can dostum,
birbirimize yol olmak lazım.

Sun rises, sun sets, yet,
civilization sees no dawn.
How long shall we stay savage,
how long shall we mock and mourn!

In mocking each other we mock ourselves,
In celebrating death we forget to live.
How long will these divisions take preference,
When will we hail the helm of life's steed!

You keep moving on auto-pilot like a robot,
either nudged by nature or by nurture.
When will you grow out of nature and nurture,
when, I ask you, will you be your own master!

Either you dance to the politicians,
or you dance to your ancestors.
For once, and for the first time in history,
let us dance, not against, but with each other.

Be the proof of integration,
when prejudice is the tradition.
Devise your own inclusive destiny,
when heritage is rooted in division.

Long have we stayed divided,
long have we worshipped stupidity.
It is time to grow out of ignorance,
it is time to muster some expansivity.

We expand, therefore we are -
we explore, therefore we grow.
Take away the will to expand,
and you sentence yourself to woe.

To live we must expand,
to survive it's not that important.
So the question is, do you wanna live,
or just crawl a few decades as insect?

Today's revolution is tomorrow's civilization,
today's responsibility is tomorrow's reformation.
Today's accountability is tomorrow's tradition,
today's mutation is tomorrow's expansion.

Mutate your mind from cruelty to kindness,
and I shall give you assimilation.
Rise above self-help to unself-help,
and I shall give you civilization.

Quieres vivir para siempre,
Walk like un buen ayudante.
Anybody can take, take, and take,
My motto is to give my life away.

Part 2

8

Part 2

It is by giving, we get to live,
by losing the self, we find the self,
Sacrifice is the highway to immortality.
Neither intellect, nor ignorance, what's needed
is uncompromisable collectivity.

Dendrons of Dynamite,
Axons of Asphalt,
Corazón de Kevlar -
That's how we move the world,
That's how we emerge as humanizer.

Heart anchored in love needs no lesson
on standing up and taking responsibility.
Feet stranger to the course of love
ain't no human feet but those of centipede.

Those who are moved by love,
can move the whole world.
No world is human world,
that is not moved by love.

Those who are moved by the world,
can move the whole world.
Those who are moved by nothing,
are but residents of the underworld.

Love the world or not,
it doesn't matter to the world.
But does it not bother you to live on,
without love, without light, without concord!

Can you live with yourself,
with all the hate you've inherited?
Is it not time yet to forfeit the burden,
Is it not human to disown your inheritance!

Don't listen to the world outside,
don't listen to the world behind.
None of it is alive in the present,
all of it is remnant of a long gone night.

Defy yourself to defy the night,
defy yourself to defy the day.
Till you wake up from the curse of heritage,
night and day both keep the light away.

Nobody has seen the night,
nobody has seen the day.
All we see is effect of desire,
light dawns the being who
throws the self away.

It ain't enough to love music,
time has come for us to be the music.
It ain't enough to love what's beautiful,
time has come to pour out some beautiful magic.

It ain't a shame to be good,
it ain't a shame to be kind.
It ain't a shame to keep the windows open,
it ain't a shame to not stay blind.

It ain't a shame to be free,
it ain't a shame to reject prejudice.
It ain't a shame to despise death 'n despair,
it ain't a shame to try 'n live.

Life is poetry no poet can write,
life is science no scientist can grasp.
Life is to be lived for life's sake,
not autopsied like differential calculus.

Live life like you mean to live,
value the living more than you value the dead.
Till you learn to unlearn the old ways of life,
you won't know what's human, what's unsuited.

Part 3

Part 3

Real education starts
with uneducation.
Once you understand this,
you'll understand education.

When culture is code for division,
You gotta be uncultured to find assimilation.
When hagiographies are passed on as heritage,
To be heretic is the first course of action.

But be a heretic for the right reason,
not simply to seek attention.
To rebel for no reason is just
another kind of authoritarianism.

Infidelity is the first sign of religion,
Disbelief is the sign of practical divinity.
Birth of a question is the birth of understanding,
To question division is to practice humanity.

Division is the antithesis of humanity,
Oneness is humanity in practice.
Those who look human but live divided,
are but a walking wasteland of prejudice.

Yeni bir insan ol, yeni bir hayat yaz.
İnsanın hakikatini insan yazmalı,
İnsanın nasibini insan yazmalı,
İnsanın hikayesi insan yazmalı,
İnsanın ilacı insan olmalı.

Instead of being chained to the dead,
Let us be each other's roots.
Be a garland that celebrates life,
Instead of a hangman's noose.

It may not be easy, for we've not evolved for peace,
Every step of the way nature will tempt us to be cruel.
If we can resist it with our still feeble civilized will,
Then only shall we rise with peace unstoppable.

For the impossible fiction of peace to be real,
what is needed is an impossible peacemaker.
Peace is an act of civic duty,
not a task for the world leaders.

World leaders don't make the world go round,
everyday, ordinary citizens do that.
Awake, arise, and be the uncommon commoner -
Curb the bias, carve the world.

Beings and bias should never go together,
and yet, beings and bias will always go together.
Because perception is but rooted in biases,
Human brain's prime directive is bias manufacture.

Let's take the concept of alpha male for example,
it exists only in a world of animals and morons.
The civilized don't bother with primitive constructs,
only mindless savages chase after such stoneage notions.

We are so primitively biased to our bone that,
we even measure leadership with primitive concepts.
We still proudly associate guns with valor,
as a bunch of hypocrites who crave for violence.

Every gentleman is alpha male,
whereas most alpha males are just jerks.
Focus on being gentle, being humble,
instead of obsessing over a prehistoric construct.

Be gentle, be humble,
let not animals turn you animal.
Remember that, no matter the gender,
leadership means firstly, service to the fallen.

Part 4

United Nations cannot bring peace,
only united humans can.
Be shredded to your very core,
but never let barbarians do harm.

Wield your wounds like crown,
Savor your scars like chocolate.
Wounds may turn animals bitter,
They usher humans into gentleness.

Some rise from darkness as walking doom,
Then there are some who never rise at all.
Some rise from darkness cold as dead,
Then there are those who emerge as a brave dawn.

Generalization never brings understanding,
Integrity of society lies on individual integrity.
Neither nature nor nurture can define your destiny,
Unless you submit to their convenient authority.

Though early studies of evolutionary biology
exposed the dilemma of nature and nurture,
we have come a long way since then,
modern Neuroscience has revealed much more.

Regardless of modern neuroscientific evidence,
we are still stuck with naturing and nurturing,
because, the dilemma of nature and nurture
fits quite well with society's binary thinking.

Binarism is the ultimate social norm,
for we're fond of a black and white world.
But reality is rather a grey dimension,
which we despise, as it takes too much effort.

To fathom greyness the mind needs to be free,
which means acting against our tendency of allegiance,
Yet social psyche is rooted in our instinct of allegiance,
we talk freedom but subconsciously we crave obedience.

Evolutionarily we are conditioned against freethinking,
Society further strengthens this evolutionary instinct.
The appearance of our society might have changed a lot,
Internally like all animals we still behave tribalistic.

You should adapt your customs to the people you love,
instead of forcing them to adapt to your customs.
You should adapt your customs to the world of today,
instead of forcing the world to adapt to the past.

No matter the age of your skin,
in spirit be a rejuvenated youth.
Stand ready to discard the most revered custom,
if it doesn't aid in the healing of wounds.

Many grow old without growing young,
Youth is not a number, but a state of awareness.
When awareness overcomes the tradition of rigidity,
that is the awakening of youthfulness.

Then again, as I said, it's a grey, grey world -
things are never as they appear to be.
Quite often, youth goes side by side with arrogance,
just like aging goes side by side with rigidity.

What's needed is a balance between old and young,
we need rejuvenation of youth and wisdom of age.
At the same time we gotta denounce all arrogance,
while we dismantle rigidity's every last trace.

Ultimately we gotta rise
above the duality of youth and age.
Beyond the dilemma of young and old,
we gotta be whole, alive and brave.

Part 5

Part 5

Insight is not a constant,
insight is rather a spectrum.
At the beginning dualities rule,
deeper you dive, dualities disappear.

Nonduality is the better name of clarity,
which has no relation to numeral mortality.
Mortality may well be defined by numbers,
it is sacrifice that defines immortality.

So forget all that nonsense of age and youth,
Be a human and do something radical for humanity.
Live life like you actually, genuinely intend to live,
instead of crawling through the sewers of ancestry.

Be the pedestrian of a new dawn,
encourage your children to surpass you.
Never ever pass on death disguised as heritage,
infect them with the drive to reshape the world anew.

Never force your kids to be toppers,
Toppers never change the world.
Instill a sense of curiosity instead,
so they can dare to find unfound answers.

To dare the undare-able question,
To bear the unbearable burden,
To brave the unbrave-able justice,
To face the unface-able kraken.

This is the quest of the alive human,
while the dead live in an empty castle.
When confronted with barbarian prejudice,
convert yourself into a bulldozer impossible.

Birds never know if the sun will rise,
yet they sing everyday right before dawn.
And sure enough the sun emerges,
defeating the most ominous mourn.

Be the herald of impossible light,
even amidst the worries of souls most weary.
The darkness of the world may not be your fault,
to light up the world is your existential duty.

Peace is an act of pain - to have peace
you must be willing to bear pain.
Love is an act of pain - you won't know love
if all you care about is gain.

The world cares not about your pain,
still can you care for the world's pain?
In a paradigm paved by and for psychopaths,
can you be the glaringly anomalous love-lane?

We live in a world where the abundance of one
is predicated on the bankruptcy of another.
Let all such coldness and hypocrisy end with you,
Be the real sapiens standing as the equalizer.

Nature conditioned us to be psychopaths,
Society conditions us to be sociopaths.
It is time to emerge as crazy lovers,
It is time we carve a genuine human path.

None of us are raised as citizens of a sanctuary,
We are raised to be residents of a sanitarium.
Isn't it time we grow out of such convenient tradition,
Isn't it time we become each other's asylum!

Until we wake up to a life of dignity, it's no life -
Until all of us are free, none of us are free.
Until each face reflects the smile of another,
we'll keep confusing self-centricity with liberty.

Part 6

It's the welfare of society that matters,
not the opinion of society run by populism.
If you only care for the opinion of society,
you won't ever witness equality and integration.

It is a shortsighted world drunk on populism,
and you have to do something impossible to be noticed.
But if what you do is only to be noticed by others,
then you are the reason for the world being populist.

I never dreamt of becoming a humanitarian beacon,
or that I would end up humanizing the sciences.
All I ever wanted was to lift the world above divisions,
everything else is nothing more than a happy accident.

Eyes on ambition,
feet on the ground.
Hands on heart,
and mind unbound.

That's how we work the mission,
that's how the mission works us.
That's how we transcend the jungle,
into the dimension of impossible stars.

I am not gifted,
I am just undivided.
I am just a plain human,
who outgrew divisiveness.

There is no such thing as gift,
it is all just simple uniqueness.
Every single being is endowed
with the potential for greatness.

By calling potential, gift,
society keeps it from becoming norm.
By calling goodness, altruism,
society keeps it from becoming norm.

By calling accountability as activism,
society maintains its integrity of indifference.
By branding plain humanness as humanitarianism,
society maintains its predominant coldness.

A flower doesn't bloom to impress others,
it blooms because that is its role
upon the fabric of nature.
Human accountable needs neither
approval nor admiration,
an ocean's role is to nourish
the planet with life and laughter.

Try not to fathom the ocean
by a glass or two of its water.
Leave behind all head-butting,
and be one with the ocean fervor.

You must kill yourself before you know yourself,
you are your own impediment to understanding.
So long as the self is aloof on a pedestal,
all task by the ape is dehumanizing.

To know the self you must forget the self,
To find the self you must lose the self.
Focus on learning curves, not burning carbs -
Focus on expansion, not on contracting descent.

Plenty curves on the outside, but all dry on the inside,
that is not a living human, but a lifeless statue.
Access to knowledge, with no access to heart,
is no different from a mule bearing a lot of books.

All the books are useless,
if they don't elevate the heart.
Then again, books don't elevate the heart,
it's the heart that,
with some aid from books,
elevates the world.

Part 7

Part 7

We all need some sort of asylum,
and only the heart can give us asylum.
Head is the greatest aid that the heart has got,
hence it is imperative, they work in unison.

Heart is to lead the world,
head is to aid the heart.
Backbone must boost the being,
one who is run not by hate, but love.

When a human is run by love, they'll feel choked
by the very thought of exclusively sectarian identity.
Human never says, I prefer division - I prefer disorder,
Human always says, I am inclusion - I am harmony.

I submit to no segregation,
for I am a living sapiens.
I submit to no derangement,
for I am but a beacon of existence.

Exist or not for long, I don't care,
I only care about existing as human.
What's the point of all this intellect,
if we cannot be each other's asylum!

Life begins at the end of your selfish zone,
Heart begins outside the monocultural prison.
Divinity begins at the end of the doctrinal zone,
Existence begins at the end of sectarianism.

Till integration becomes life,
life will but lead to disintegration.
Till assimilation becomes existence,
existence will cause nothing but extinction.

Existence without integration
is an exploitation of life-force,
yet segregation comes easy to us,
while integration feels nonsense woke.

Humanity is conditioned against integration,
To be integrated we gotta go against convenience.
We gotta be willing to renovate our whole outlook,
if we ever wish to stand up as actual sapiens.

Fabric of the human space is predicated
upon our inclusive acts in everyday life.
Neither law nor policy can ensure inclusion,
if conscience is too malnourished to value life.

When the citizens only look human,
when the limbs are lacking in spirit,
all the constitutions can't make them walk,
all the institutions can't bring uplift.

Too many words, too little meaning!
Too much policy, too little accountability!
Too much philosophy, too little common sense!
Too much government, too little civic duty!

Politicians have thrown people out of government,
Philosophers have thrown humanity out of philosophy.
Scientists have thrown the society out of science,
Preachers have thrown plain goodness out of divinity.

They are not to blame for our rotten fabric,
because these people are none but us.
Unless we wake up from our sleep of greed,
our indifference will keep wreaking disasters.

When the world runs on greed and inequality,
you can do nothing civilized with convenience.
You know, what's better than following the map!
It is to chart the map to territory uncharted.

Part 8

If the mind is oblivious to the light within,
all the outside menorahs are meaningless.
If the heart doesn't shine with a Christly spirit,
all the gifts hanging on trees are worthless.

You know why most menorahs nowadays have
nine branches even though Hanukkah lasts eight days!
It is to hold the ninth candle that sacrifices itself
to light up the lives of those lamenting in darkness.

Let the festivities take away the darkness.
May each festival wake us up to increased inclusivity!
Let kindness be the byword of everyday life.
Let no hate taint the sacred inner sanctum of humanity.

Hate thrives on ignorance, biases and prejudice,
Get hold of these and you just might conquer hate.
But mind you, this is no act of sheer intellect,
Conquest of hate is but an act of wholeness.

Without wholeness intellect turns dry and does harm,
Without wholeness faith becomes a choir of divide.
Without wholeness science runs cold and destroys all,
Without wholeness mind remains animal uncivilized.

Listen not to my words,
but to my voice if you may.
Look not at the person,
but at the idea if you may.

Seek not the lesson in my lectures,
my life is my lesson to you, if you may.
Seek me not in a nation or religion,
seek me in your heart, if you may.

If there is no wholeness in your heart,
even a billion of my words won't make you whole.
But the point is, wholeness lies in every heart,
yet, to wield it feels like a task impossible.

To achieve the impossible
you gotta do the inconvenient.
And nothing is more inconvenient than
acknowledging the follies of biases unsapient.

Often intelligence comes encapsulated in bias,
which is far worse than the impact of ignorance.
Ignorance is easy to notice, for it is straightforward,
difficult is to shake the cold stupidity of intelligence.

Stupidity is the default mode of human thinking,
initially even I was a bit rough around the edges.
The facts that I spoke of still remain just as true but,
the way I presented them lacked a certain humaneness.

But that's what is called the evolution of human mind,
if there is no change in thinking it's a sign of stagnation.
Fools are too blinded by ego to realize their follies,
the wise accept stupidity as a crucial part of expansion.

Back when I wrote the treatise on gender equality,
I was very much opposed to being called a feminist.
Over time as gender equality became one of my pillars,
I realized, it's an honor to be deemed a feminist.

Just like black lives matter is a struggle of all,
the feminist movement is a struggle of humankind.
Struggle of one people is the struggle of all people,
we can't uphold justice till we leave all barriers behind.

Intelligence doesn't necessarily expand the mind,
Often times intelligence is a hindrance to awareness.
Knowledge without heart
disconnects the soul from society,
Good intention without realization
brings a deluge of decadence.

Part 9

Acknowledge your shortcomings,
Acknowledge your narrowness.
That's how you grow up to be human,
That's how you step across intelligence.

It is just as important to step across intelligence,
as it is to step across ignorance.
It is as important to shake the arrogance of knowledge,
as it is to shake off the blind rigidity of faith.

Coldness and rigidity are the problem,
and they can come from any direction.
Unless our priority is to be a decent human,
ignorance and knowledge both will bring descension.

For example, concrete has a certain advantage,
it keeps us safe from the cruelties of the jungle.
But concrete devoid of green is a petri-dish of disease,
An hour in nature prevents a year at the hospital.

Balance is the key to a healthy life,
Balance is the key to a healthy society.
Binarism is the root of all bigotry,
Dualism is the root of disharmony.

Dualism is the root of disharmony,
yet dualism has been the norm of life.
That's why harmony is still fiction,
and the road to peace is jammed with strife.

We are all raised to think like a dualistic derriere,
it takes immense character to defy habits of heritage.
My belief is beyond error, says the shortsighted savage,
I err, I correct, I expand - says the civilized sapiens.

If you don't like the world you are born in,
build the world you wish you were born in.
If there is not a single real human around,
be the first sapiens to stand up and intervene.

But to stand up to the inhumanity outside,
you gotta stand up to the inhumanity inside first.
If you haven't grabbed hold of your own biases,
how on earth will you humanize the bigoted world!

That's why I am constantly on the lookout for my biases,
way more than I am mindful of the biases of others.
To hell with the identity I am born and raised with,
my identity is what I write
with my conscience courageous.

It's okay if you take some time
to conquer your biases.
Just make sure you don't confuse
predispositions with destiny.

Unless you are mindful
of a mind full of biases,
Biases will fool you
into behaving most mindless.

Don't take conditioning
as the ultimate condition of life.
Struggle against conditioning mustn't stop,
if it does, that's the fall of the apocalyptic night.

We have to stop looking through this lens and that,
We gotta break our habit of black and white perception.
We can do that only by contemplation of the inside,
more importantly, by ceaseless self-correction.

We've consistently failed to see the greyness of reality,
That's why, Gandhi is a beacon of peace
and Guevara of rebellion.
Gandhi's naivety buttered imperialism
disguised as nonviolence,
Guevara's suspicion cost innocent lives
in the name of revolution.

The course of revolution is a moral mine-field,
One false step, and revolution turns into terrorism!
That's the whole point of having the faculty of reason -
to regulate behavior when biases contaminate emotion.

Then again, once you start practicing reason,
you run the risk of losing emotion altogether.
Again it comes down to finding the right balance,
neither reason nor emotion, let wholeness be the driver.

Reason, emotion, backbone,
all must work hand in hand.
The one who can do that,
is the only human among the animals.

Wholeness is not some intellectual theory,
it is the foundation of a real civilization.
There is no magic, there is no law of attraction,
there is only wholeness-driven law of action.

It takes a lot of sweat, and wounds to the heart,
to rescue the world from the grovel-pit of misery.
You can pray all you like without lifting a finger,
that will lift neither you nor the fallen humanity.

Part 10

Act, act, and act again, with the
last ounce of energy in your atoms.
E=MC^2 can destroy the world,
it can also light up the human dimension.

Love adds direction to mind,
Mind adds direction to matter.
When there is a place for love in the mind,
all things civilized will rightfully appear.

But one thing I must make absolutely clear,
True love will always shatter you to pieces.
That's how love transforms ice-water into blood,
That's how love filters the humans from savages.

Broken heart is not the proof of a failed lover,
Broken heart is the test of a true lover.
Broken heart wakes you up to the worth of heart,
It is in brokenness that wholeness is discovered.

Wholeness is the lifeblood of civilization,
Wholeness paves the way for assimilation.
Wholeness brings all the trust that we need,
It is in wholeness that we find transformation.

It takes a lot of heart to build trust,
Even more to keep the trust.
But what if both hearts are in pieces,
How will they ever overcome their past!

The answer is really quite simple, and yet,
It is the last revelation to be crystal clear.
Seek not for perfection but for the being,
Broken in heart but intact in character.

The road to joy is paved with broken hearts,
Broken heart is something to cherish not mourn.
Heart not broken is a heart devoid of life,
That's how the pieces of two fit together as one.

You know why we are all in pieces -
so that we may find wholeness in each other.
This is why integration is no bookish theory,
we are human only when we stand together.

Togetherness is the byword of human life,
without it we ain't no human no matter the tech.
But the only way we can make it the norm is,
if the bravehearts are ready to sacrifice their existence.

Part 11

This is what my Christmas looks like,
And my Hanukkah, Ramadan, Diwali 'n Onam.
I don't get to celebrate any of the festivals,
So that the world can, without discrimination.

Each day that I miss out on a festival
to wipe out hate, is not short of a festivity.
Unless a few mighty mortals give up their life,
the world can never have love, life and liberty.

No tengo fiesta, no tengo vida,
porque soy responsable de la humanidad.
I have no festival, I have no life,
unification of humankind es mi guerra.

Integration is my muse,
Integration is my mission.
Till integration is the way of life,
There is no rest for the transformer human.

Poet has no power over the muse,
it's the muse who powers the poet.
Best of poetry is an act of selfless care,
as the poet pens the pain through hopelessness.

Human is the muse,
Human is the mission.
Human is the poetry,
Human is walking integration.

Humanity is but a reflection of human,
When the individual is human so is humanity.
Individual means, a person who is indivisible,
Humanity is but a concoction of human and unity.

To unite this divided world,
first you gotta be indivisible inside.
If you are still a slave to ideology,
you have no right to talk of peace and light.

Light is not the absence of differences,
Light is the absence of differentiation.
Peace is not the absence of conflict,
Peace is the absence of condescension.

Condescension has been the bane of our existence,
Most times we do it without even being aware.
We're conditioned to be condescending,
not conscientious,
Whoever conquers their conditioning
conquers the world.

An expert knows they are expert in nothing,
The non-expert behaves like an expert in everything.
The more you learn, the more you actually unlearn,
True wisdom puts an end to all traits condescending.

That is where wisdom differs from intellect -
Intellect only builds the house,
warmth and wisdom make it a home.
That's where insight differs from intelligence -
Intelligence furnishes a planet with comfort,
insight makes it a civilized dorm.

Intellect untempered by love,
goes hand in hand with bigotry.
Unless you are cautious of intellect,
you are headed for catastrophe.

Tame your intellect like
you tame your ignorance.
Tame your beliefs, because
those are infested with biases.

Even intellect is not impervious to biases,
In fact, biases reign all over your perception.
Thus, intellectuals are a different kind of ignoramus,
trapped in the purgatory of an illusion of illumination.

Part 12

Real illumination makes you aware of your stupidity,
What it doesn't do is, set you aloof from the living.
Real illumination opens your eyes to the supreme truth -
What is that truth you ask - what else, but a kind living.

Good deeds through the day
makes you sleep well at night.
Good deeds throughout life
makes you die well with a smile.

Fear not the death of life,
fear if you must, a life of death.
Be afraid not, of living while alive,
instead of being crippled by death.

The more dead you are inside,
the more you are afraid of death.
Those who are actually alive,
have too much to do to be frightened.

As I said, good deeds through the day
makes you fall asleep happy and content.
And what is death, if not the ultimate
sleep of eternal unawareness!

But the point is, to live life
you gotta be aware of life.
If you spend life without awareness,
you are already more dead and alive.

Stay not dead no more,
Stay not lost in unawareness.
Wake up and be lost in life,
Be happy, be sad - live life to the fullest.

To be happy is human,
To be sad is human.
To make another smile
despite your agony,
is practical divination.

Everybody fears hell, all they
want is a heaven of convenience.
Only the brave can dare to break
into hell to rescue the innocent.

If you want to change your life,
it's not gonna be convenient.
If you want to change the world,
it's gonna be even more inconvenient.

Nothing worthwhile is ever convenient,
Nothing alive ever exists in convenience.
Death is the ultimate sanctuary of convenience,
and yet, to live is to dance through inconvenience.

To be destroyed for life, isn't a shame,
Shame is to destroy life in fear of death.
To be disgraced for love, isn't a shame,
Shame is to disgrace life by acts of hate.

Yaşamak için berbat olmak ayıp değil.
Eğer korkuyorsa, yaşamadan ölmekten kork.
Sevmek için sarhoş olmak ayıp değil.
Eğer korkuyorsa, aşksız akıllı olmaktan kork.

You won't know what life is,
Till you die a thousand times.
Once you break the spell of death,
Every moment you'll rise revitalized.

Once you wake up to life,
the very idea of death disappears.
The more your mind comes to life,
you lose touch with baseless fears.

Part 13

The more you expand in mind,
the smaller the world gets.
Only when you are small in mind,
the world feels like a vast 'n scary place.

That's why there are so many borders,
they treat and breed fear simultaneously.
It is like a primordial fright loop,
sustained in the name of national security.

All talk of borders inadvertently brings along
the notion of sacrifice of your side
against the atrocities of the other side.
However, the borders outside are not the problem,
the problem is that we are divided on the inside.

Once we wipe out the borders from our heart,
all external borders will lose their gravity.
Once you learn to defy the gravity of tribalism,
no barbwire can obstruct the oneness of humanity.

However, we can never be one humanity,
until we renounce all knacks of rigidity.
Unless we actually value life over tribe,
we can never foster an inclusive morality.

Using scripture to decode morality,
is like using the abacus to code iOS.
Likewise, using mere reason to decode life,
is like trading in a family for computers.

Computers do have a role in family,
But computers are not family themselves.
Just like scriptures may have a role in life,
But scriptures alone ain't life themselves.

The coming generations will sure be free,
from the stupidity of fundamentalist religiosity.
But they'll be the victim of a new stupidity, i.e.
intellectual fundamentalism or militant logicality.

And trading in one stupidity for another,
only gets us stuck in derangement eternal.
Just know, love has no proof, love is the proof,
And, love has no gospel, love is the gospel.

When love is the center of our field of vision,
All things civilized attain their rightful place.
But when we replace love with either ritual or reason,
We end up with everything except peace and wellness.

There is a gateway in my mind,
which opens from time to time and
I'm poured with some magical words.
Some call it a gift, I call it nature -
Mind is the gateway to its own universe.

All have the potential to be the gateway of love,
Yet till now tradition has kept the gateway shut.
In practice, tradition does more to connect you
to the dead, than to the living of the living world.

Our idea of neighbor doesn't extend beyond ten feet,
Because tradition has consistently failed in integration.
Integration is a cornerstone of human society,
Tradition devoid of integration
has no place in civilization.

So I ask you - who is a neighbor?
Anybody and everybody you come across.
And I ask you - who is a family?
Anybody and everybody who lives and breathes.

Let no ancestor bind your identity behind borders,
let no heritage be a hindrance to your humanity.
If a language or culture makes you
squeamish or afraid,
it means you gotta wash your heart
with soap and sanity.

Part 14

Graveyard of Dreams
(The Sonnet)

When the heart is born in the middle of a desert,
Is it wrong for them to set out in search of water!
Or should the heart remain a handicapped patriot,
Never to realize and manifest their rightful power!

No heart is ever known by the land they are born in,
Heart is known by the light it pours out into the world.
I say, cut off all allegiance to the intolerant desert,
And seek out the land where your roots are watered.

Heart's allegiance is only to light,
not to some puny tribe,
Land your feet where they greet you
with garland, not shackles.
Those who continue to peddle patriotism
to guilt trap the genius,
Are the last people to deserve
exclusive rights to light universal.

Seek out an environment conducive to your light,
Instead of being chained to the graveyard of dreams.
Wield your light with all your conviction and dignity,
And you'll illuminate all, even the dreamkilling fiends.

Rigidity is an impediment to growth,
Tribalism is a threat to harmony.
Nationalism is the greatest threat to peace,
Sectarianism is crime against humanity.

Tribalism is a violation of life,
it is a violation of everything civilized.
Sugarcoat it all you want, that won't
take the stink out of the carcass uncivilized.

So far we've been playing pretend sapiens,
for sapiens sectarian is no sapiens.
Till we muster the guts to reject tribalism,
we have no right to the title of sapiens.

Sapiens ain't a species,
sapiens ain't a life-form.
Sapiens is a promise,
sapiens is a uniform.

Measure of a sapiens ain't appearance,
measure of a sapiens ain't etiquette.
Measure of a sapiens lies in the spirit,
the spirit of motion across divisiveness.

As I once said, it ain't enough to look human,
You gotta feel, think and behave human.
And there is no greater impediment to our humanity,
than our innately primeval tendency of divisionism.

Oneness is the better name of humanity,
but it's achievable by nobody else but the lover.
Distance is but a myth, a sign of love's absence -
Be drunk in love, and lo, all distance disappears.

You call it grandiosity, I call it self-determination,
You call it God complex, I call it accountability.
Long enough we've fought like morons over fiction,
Isn't it time to recognize each other's inner divinity!

But I guess you won't know what I mean,
for it takes a sapiens to know a sapiens.
What does a good looking baboon know
of the intricacies of civilized sentience!

Justice doesn't happen because you wash your hands,
Peace doesn't drop from the sky as you keep binging.
Justice is raised only by civilized sentience,
bearing sleepless nights, and heartaches unending.

Part 15

Just Need to Be Human
(The Sonnet)

You don't need to be an arab to stand by
the muslims, you just need to be human.
You don't need to be an immigrant to stand up
against hate crime, you just need to be human.

You don't need to be a woman to stand up
to misogyny, you just need to be human.
You don't need to be a queer to stand up
to phobia, you just need to be human.

You don't need to be colored to defy
discrimination, you just need humanity.
You just need to be not stupid enough,
to confuse diversity with pathology.

Every person we meet is our neighbor.
We cannot exist as human beings,
till we wipe each other's tears.

There is no rest for the real human,
till the last drop of tear is wiped out.
There is no sleep for the real human,
till all suffering is wiped out.

There is no justice for the real human,
till all injustice is brought to an end.
There is no life for the real human,
till all lives live equally well.

This is not a concept,
this is not an ideology.
Those who confuse inclusion with ism,
are the root of all inequality.

Ism is the prison,
Ism is impediment.
Take the I beyond the ism,
And lo, you are sapient!

Let us just be human,
this year, and every year.
With this hate-defying hope,
I wish you a happy new year.

Every day, you choose to defy hate, is new year,
Every day, you defy discrimination, is a new dawn.
Her yer evim benim, her insan ailem,
Every person is family, every place is my home.

Discrimination defied is civilization unfolded,
Discrimination defied is humanity upheld.
Oneness realized is light unfolded,
Oneness realized is peace upheld.

Peace is not a theory,
It is theory only when we live by theory.
Crave for peace like you crave for bread,
Only then shall you know harmony.

Harmony is human in action,
Peace is a person accountable.
Unity is a heart that functions,
Justice is backbone incorruptible.

It's all very simple,
yet why does it seem so damn hard!
Because we despise all inconvenience,
we never actually bring down our guard.

Part 16

We are more concerned with guarding
ideology than preserving humanity.
We are too busy fighting over
ethical theories to practice ethicality.

It is more convenient to argue over theories,
than be the walking demonstration of practice.
Fools argue over which philosophy is the best,
the wise ignore philosophy and focus on deeds.

Fools laud the figure, forgetting the fervor,
Fools laud memorizing, without realizing.
Fools laud the structure, forgetting the spirit,
Fools laud the dead, abandoning the living.

Memorizing someone is not the same
as cherishing someone's memories.
Cherish a teacher for the spirit they possessed,
instead of making them the excuse
for doctrinal atrocities.

Disciples cause all the divisions, not the teacher,
Followers cause all corruption, not the leader.
When the individual becomes their own teacher,
Only then will the divisions disappear.

Dump all your moronic divisions,
Peace will triumph, all unbound.
Nerde yarası, orda ışığı,
Heart lost is heart found.

Unleash your unsubmission,
and character unfolds.
Once character unfolds,
civilization unfolds.

When your ancestors desecrate your character,
dump your ancestors not your character.
When tradition demands you to remain prejudiced,
better be a traitor than a divisive disaster.

Let nothing come between you and your dream,
let nothing obstruct your potential humanity.
Keep at your mission like a brakeless bulldozer,
take no notice of the insults of primitivity.

It's not selfish to run away from insult,
Better run away than retaliate with harm.
Even mindless cavemen have a right to live,
Even if they know not the worth of the sun.

I spent years chasing parasites, begging for help,
all I received was ridicule and cold shoulder.
So I speak not a word of the land I was born in,
some wounds are too big for even a saint to bear.

So, stay or run - do as you like,
Do whatever helps you shine your light.
Places are myths, only the person is real,
Person is the source of all light and sight.

No one civilized asks the sun, where do you come from?
Sun's light is too sacred to be desecrated with division.
It's only the savages who are burdened with trivialities.
Nature of a question reflects the nature of the person.

Fools seek identity in ancestry,
The wise build their identity with sweat and blood.
Savages ask questions of race, religion and nationality,
while the peace incarnate rises with a civilized heart.

Be your own identity, be your own fortune,
even if all the traditions tell you otherwise.
Tradition of life is written by life itself,
let not dead tradition define your living rights.

Part 17

Rights of the living oughta be
determined only by the living.
If and when I become obsolete someday,
it's me you oughta reject, not the living.

Keep traditions in your memory,
But don't place them in your heart.
The heart belongs only to the here and now,
Don't desecrate it with backward dirt.

Where there is heart, there is hayat,
Heartless hayat is no hayat.
Call it hayat, life, or call it vida,
All of it begins across divisive dirt.

No identity is worth keeping,
if it hinders your humanity.
No life is worth living,
if it reeks of inhumanity.

Life is meant to be a vessel
for carrying goodness across time.
If all you carry is hate as heritage,
how can you ever be anyone's lifeline!

If one life isn't another's lifeline,
is it really life or death in disguise!
If a human is not a human's greatest strength,
is it really human or but an ape in disguise!

The proof of life is life itself,
Seek it not in facades and cages.
The proof of love is love itself,
Seek it not on history pages.

Proof of existence is existence itself,
Ignore it not worshipping the nonexistent.
To love is the journey, to love is destination,
Only the dead waste their life in bookish argument.

The universal reason is love,
The universal faith is love.
All else is but a faint echo,
Driving us away from love.

Taking the echo for the source,
the living heart turns bitter stone.
The sky above knows no east and west,
only the bugs beneath insist on separation.

Taking the chaff for the seed,
the creature cripples its own nourishment.
Taking the husk for the heart,
even the learned forfeits their sapience.

Lower you fall, more divided you get,
Higher you fly, more you find assimilation.
Animal tradition is rooted in exclusion,
Human tradition oughta be rooted in expansion.

Go seek love, so it may kill you to your core.
You cannot come to life, till you're dead to yourself.
You are your greatest impediment to love and life,
Seek the walls within, then smash them to pieces.

Till the inanimate matter chooses to die,
Mindful life cannot be born.
Till you blind your eyes to all blindness,
Real sight of civilization will never dawn.

Brush off all backwardness as blind men's folly,
And yes, when I say men, I mean men alone.
Leave all stale ways behind, including patriarchy,
Lo, the desert world turns lush green on its own.

Part 18

Leave all intolerance and fear behind,
Let no moron infect you with jungle fever.
Even if that moron happens to be a relative,
Call them out if they violate human welfare.

We have gotten so hooked on ancestral fear,
we've lost all vision of a world without hate.
Forget vision, we lack even the common sense,
to tell superstition from actual knowledge.

They say travel broadens the mind,
and the world is crawling with such myths
transmitted from blind to blind.
If travel indeed broadened the mind,
the rich would be the least small-minded people alive.

Savages stay savage even if
they travel to the moon.
Civilized soul needs no travel
to journey to dawn from doom.

Journey o traveler, journey inside -
journey from yourself to yourself.
All the outward travels are worthless,
if the heart keeps on its hateful yell.

Heart is the gate out of the hate,
Heart is the path out of the prison.
If you are still worried, come, hold my hand,
I'll walk by you till you feel all one.

I am not your teacher, I am not your guide,
But we mess up less, when we mess up together.
Hold my hand, as we chart the course of light,
Together we are creator, divided we are disaster.

One heart joins another,
Thus the world comes to life.
Heart is a miracle, not merchandise,
Place the heart above all else in life.

So, come, let's take the leap across fear,
with an act of intolerance-defying acceptance.
End of intolerance is the birth of a human,
beyond fear lies peace - taming fear stands sapiens.

I am but a farmer of assimilation, and I know,
I won't get to see the saplings turn savannah.
But someday humankind will stand up and say,
Glory be to them, who toiled for our humanistana!

Plant, my friend - plant the sapling
of love even if it is doomsday.
Duty of the human is to aid humanity,
not to scheme an entire life away.

Enough with judgment, enough with manipulation,
Enough with all those tricks to win arguments!
For once let us sit together without presupposition,
So we can finally set sail through the healing process.

Healing is an act of a pure heart,
There can be no healing if the heart
is overtaken by a scheming head.
Healing begins when you submit to love,
and stand ready to be reborn in acceptance.

Healing begins when the human is born,
but most humans are never actually born,
for they spend their life as slave to stereotypes,
thus they never get to be actually human.

Healing begins with the human,
Human who isn't afraid of humans.
Animals may be scared of their own kind,
Such behavior doesn't suit us humans.

Part 19

Heal, don't hate - love, don't loath,
Every soul alive is a soul wounded.
Human history is a history of hate,
Isn't it time to dump all that torment!

We are born to be bees, yet
for whatever reason, we end up as flies.
Defy all norms that devoid you of honey,
Determine not your destiny by the stupidity of flies.

When you hate others, you really hate yourself,
Hate is the greatest impediment to the light of heart.
Unless you learn to say 'No', to the heritage of hate,
That very heritage will keep dragging us down to dirt.

Rise above all that nonsense of heritage,
so that you may unfold real civilized traditions.
Unless you stand as traitor to the animals,
you can never be a transformer to the humans.

For a million morons acting in hate,
driven by fear, bigotry and intolerance,
there will rise ten Naskars acting as human,
driven by the prime directive of humanness.

I choose to be a traitor to the dead,
So I can be an ally to the living.
Sometimes no choice is actually a choice,
of siding with habits most damaging.

For every existence wasted in unexistence,
Civilization is set back a hundred years.
Object of existence is the unfolding of life,
Not the worship of spiritless structures.

Quit the contraction, start the construction,
Set out as sailors in the course of unity.
Quit the paralysis, start the osmosis,
Disinfect the world with your fearless electricity.

Our world is our design,
Our life is our design.
It's time for mind to start minding,
No myth is master to the mind.

Jellyfish call it karma,
The juggernaut only knows unselfish duty.
Cowards leave all to kismet, fate or destiny,
Creators wield life as an instrument of causality.

Be the cause of a civilized world,
Not an effect of uncivilized tradition.
Be the reason for future gratitude,
Not the excuse for regret and regression.

Life is either a vow or void,
All depends on the mind at helm.
When the mind reigns over its reality,
No dead divide can take a single step.

You are the vow nature made to herself -
the vow of an impossible spirit -
impossible, because if anything -
you are but conditioned for defeat.

So the question is,
will you accept defeat,
like our ape ancestors did,
or be the first spark of the human spirit!

Spirit is the root of the person,
Stronger the spirit, stronger the person.
If the spirit never forgets that
their very existence is a vow to be kept,
no jungle can dehumanize such a person.

Part 20

They say, we don't live in a jungle no more,
But the reality is quite the opposite.
Only the shape of the jungle outside has changed,
But the jungle inside remains just as primitive.

You can take the ape out of the jungle,
but you can't take the jungle out of the ape.
Unless we acknowledge this simple fact of evolution,
We the apes will never ever grow up to be sapient.

The fire of sapiens burns brighter
in the presence of heart,
whereas it turns stale and goes out soon,
where there is no sign of heart.

So before you know you are animal,
Know why you wanna know you are animal.
From that basic knowing of the prime intent,
Shall dawn the first glint of human incorruptible.

Burn the heart in its own fire,
drown the heart in its own ocean,
so that the heart may emerge purified
of its own old dirt and delusions.

When life is rooted in delusion,
no UN can instill peace amongst such life.
Life must take charge of its own peace,
refusing to accept any reality that vilifies life.

Mark you, I am not talking about illogicality,
I am talking about inhumanity.
It is okay for the humans to be illogical,
But no human must end up as vessel of inhumanity.

Logicality is no measure of humanity,
If it were, computers would be most human.
Measure of a human is concern for human welfare,
So long as you feel another's pain, you are human.

Feel, my friend - feel with your whole being,
Trash all intellectual nonsense of detachment.
If life is afraid to be attached to life,
It is not life but derangement.

Either live or don't,
there is no playing safe.
Vegetables chase after security,
Incorruptibles know only to live,
come drought, drain, hail or rain.

Ambition in Motion
(The Sonnet)

Come hell or high water,
Never let caution cripple your feet.
Better to fall hard and learn a lesson,
Than speculate forever with couched feet.

Everything I've achieved is by trial and error,
There was no handbook to aid my mission.
Maps to known paths are available plenty,
But there is no map to uncharted destination.

You are the handbook to your ambition,
Not your background or family treasures.
If you persist long enough, at some point,
Your persistence will outrun your failures.

Better fail than frozen - failure is the foundation.
Failure is the first sign of ambition in motion.

Part 21

Behind every glorious success,
there is a thousand heartbreaking failures.
Behind every act of creation,
there is a thousand disasters.

Behind every triumph,
there is a thousand tragedy.
Behind every proud dawn,
there is unimaginable ominosity.

Failure is ambition in motion,
Heartbreak is love in motion.
Question is knowledge in motion,
Revolution is reform in motion.

Heart breaking is heart in the making.
Speak through the break, and break through the speech,
then will you find life's calling.

The more your sight expands,
the more all divides disappear.
As pain and gain all merge together,
in their place the vision will appear.

You are the vision,
You are the visitor.
Be the scribe of society,
Or there will be only blood,
where there is water.

Wield your will like a time-space instrument,
Jump-start the world with your photons of conscience.
Because if you sit still like the rest of the animals,
The oceans will be flooded
with the blood of the innocent.

Let your reputation be ruined,
Abandon all your fragility.
Unless you are ready to be ruined for reform,
We are stuck with this counterfeit society.

Walk past your injury,
Let no affliction turn you bitter.
It's an animal's prerogative to be harsh and cruel,
Bitterness is most unbecoming on human character.

Bitterness begets bitterness -
Bitterness is a lie, don't be a liar.
Stare into the eyes of bitterness
with the smile of a thousand suns,
and slowly but surely
all bitter blood will turn into water.

Do not be yet another pawn
in the paradigm of bitterness,
do not be a regular contributor
to the wickedness weekly.
In a world where bitterness
is the lifeblood of all narrative,
be the first one standing as benevolent anomaly.

Hand of human is the hand of god,
Nobody is gonna intervene if not us.
Our screw-up is our screw-up,
Either we unscrew ourselves,
or we'll keep going in reverse.

For that you gotta find the entrance to yourself,
so that you can do some spring cleaning.
Self humanized is society humanized,
A civilized society is nothing but
a self forever civilizing.

Forget all the polishing,
smash the whole damn thing that you call identity.
Smash every bit that you call you,
and without a convenient host to carry the disease,
society will fail to continue
its posh and primal inhumanity.

Don't be a pawn in the shenanigans of savages,
You are a human, stand your ground with conviction.
A million years unfold from a single moment,
A million miracles manifest from a single action.

To renounce inaction is to work the miracle,
To renounce indifference is to be sentient.
Renounce the society as it is,
so you can build the society as it oughta be -
gentle, not gruesome - amiable, not arrogant.

I am attracted to humility,
while arrogance repels me.
Repel not the weary traveller,
Often we judge another 'cause
we don't wanna be judged any.

Often arrogance is a defense mechanism
against the possibility of judgment.
Though it sounds righteous, most times
it makes us the evil we try to prevent.

Whether others judge you or not,
is not your concern whatsoever.
Make sure you don't become a jerk,
in trying to repel jerkish behavior.

Let them judge all they want,
Let it not ruin your innocent amiability.
Arrogance is but a form of bitterness,
And bitterness is a lot of things, but not humanity.

Stand your ground and exude
strength through conviction.
But keep yourself in check at all times,
lest you become yet another specimen
of modern degeneration.

Be the new generation
with renewed conviction of collectivity,
not just recurrent degeneration.
Wear your clothes differently from
your ancestors or not, that doesn't matter,
what matters is, you wear your mind
devoid of discrimination.

Recycling is a good thing,
but you cannot recycle something
that is no longer conducive to life.
Likewise, recycle traditions of the past
that still can aid life and society,
but not those traditions that are no more
compatible with the new way of life.

Instead of treating people as objects,
born to be servant of tradition,
treat tradition as objects that are
meant to serve the human being.
If this doesn't strike as a simple act of life,
problem is not tradition, but the human being.

Grow up, already - not in body, but in mind,
grow up, so you may learn to value life.
Life that places attention on trivialities
instead of life, is not life but demise.

Person is tradition supreme,
Person is the providence.
Whatever there can ever be,
Person is the source sentience.

Shatter free from social somnolence,
Shake yourself awake from nostalgic nausea.
Your reputation is not your responsibility,
Your duty is, not to give in to snobbish bulimia.

Part 23

The concept of reputation is useless,
for animals only applaud animality.
In the middle of this jungle if you wanna be human,
you gotta get rid of all populist fantasy.

Popularity is no measure of a human,
Measure of a human lies in character.
Character is measured by principles,
not from books, but those that act as spirit lifter.

Person without principle is flesh without fervor,
Being without backbone is bag full of wind.
Brain without benevolence is muscle without mission,
Hands without heart are tentacles of a fiend.

Mindful mind is the only mind,
Mindless mind is but mockery.
Being that isn't aware of being,
is its own biggest enemy.

Be aware of the being you are,
Be mindful of the mind you got.
Be heartful when your hands unfold,
Brave it smiling through times of muck.

Brave is not, to feel not weak,
Brave is to keep going, despite weakness.
Awareness is not, to be not unaware,
Highest awareness is to be aware of our unawareness.

Are you aware when you are behaving unaware,
If you are, then there is a sliver of chance,
that you might be able to defy your conditioning.
But if you are never aware of the way you behave,
all the philosophies won't suffice
to treat humankind's inhuman inkling.

Be brave, but more than that, be aware -
bravery comes chasing when there is awareness.
Awareness makes you brave and accountable,
Accountability fills you further up
with bravery and awareness.

As I said countless times,
with the rise of realization,
separation between concepts disappears.
It is only when you are analyzing from outside,
that the elements of experience appear separate.

For example - when you can tell head from heart,
know that, you've got neither head nor heart.
When you can no longer tell them apart,
that's when you start to see some dawn across dirt.

Separation is the antithesis of life,
Either everything is one, or there is nothing.
Either you walk as the epitome of oneness,
Or you are nothing more than a walking bin.

When walking, keep your feet in the present,
not in the past, either in memory or identity.
Forge your identity from the fabric of today,
instead of borrowing some second-hand humanity.

Second-hand identity may make good fodder for fiction,
But they are most lethal to real life and society.
Be your own person, not just a photocopy of yesterday,
If this seems too much,
you are the cause of all inhumanity.

All inhumanity starts with the second-hand human -
when new humans actually act new, brutality fades.
But when second-hand humanity is an object of pride,
brutality gets refurbished decades after decades.

It takes just one generation to put
an end to the transference of inhumanity.
If you stand as wall between your child's future
and the inhuman practices of the past, automatically
the world ushers into an era of practicing humanity.

Part 24

Immunize yourself against the virus of tradition,
so that you do not pass on the disease to your children.
Once you are immunized, you'll finally gain the insight,
to tell the good from the barbarian bits of tradition.

Is tradition really a virus, one wonders!
What else can you call it, when all through history
the sole purpose of tradition has been the preservation
of one culture, separated from the rest of the world!

In short, we gotta humanize
the very definition of tradition.
And the only way to do that is
to acknowledge, there's more to life
than the habits of our ancestors.

The purpose of mind is to be a mind,
not a mouthpiece for morons.
If you cannot learn from someone
without giving up your mind,
you are the problem, not tradition.

Where there is mindless obedience, there is no learning.
Where there is heartless control, there is no life.
When you are alive, you learn what you gotta learn.
When you're dead, rituals only intensify human strife.

Rituals are supposed to lift up life,
not stand as obstacle to life.
Yet that's the only kind
of rituals we have so far,
so why not write a new range of rituals
devoid of all disregard for life.

Tradition and rituals can be a good thing,
when they are not afraid to evolve.
Rituals that don't evolve either go extinct
or cause our own extinction.

Sign of life is evolution,
Sign of death is rigidity.
Sign of human is integration,
Sign of animal is exclusivity.

Integration is the greatest religious duty,
Ascension is the greatest scientific duty.
Understanding is the greatest philosophical duty,
In short, to be human is the greatest human duty.

Make integration your tradition,
and ascension your science.
Once you take the self beyond the self,
nothing can obstruct your human radiance.

Radiance comes from things alive,
not from a bunch of rotten corpses.
If you wanna shine, first and foremost,
reject all authority of the dead.

People give power to the symbols,
people can strip them of power.
It means, doing what's unpopular,
and being hailed by the paradigm as traitor.

When you got a sore thumb, while
the other fingers are perfectly well,
it is indeed a sore thumb.
But what if the other fingers are all sore,
while the thumb alone is fit and healthy,
can it still be hailed as a sore thumb!

Even if you stick out as a sore thumb,
Stand up to inhumanity with utmost conviction.
Better to walk alone as human and be ridiculed,
than be applauded by a million inhumans.

Submit yourself to love,
nothing short of that would do.
Lovers keep doing their duty,
barkers only keep making doo-doo.

Part 25

Love is the tradition we need,
don't doctrinize it
with some puny intellect or faith.
Let love be its own description,
without resorting to lifelessness.

Religion organized is religion lost,
Love doctrinized is love ruined.
Life philosophized is life lost,
By depiction let not the depicted be ruined.

One thing you must realize -
love is not the word, neither is life.
When even the words 'love' and 'life'
fail in their purpose,
how can some puny cultures illustrate life!

Life is in every culture,
but no culture is the whole of life.
Till you feel this in your bones,
you won't know jack about civilized life.

I am Them All
(The Sonnet)

They tell me to disown my words,
or the law of christ will strike me down.
They tell me to stop writing, or else,
consciousness of krishna will bury me in ground.

I look into their eyes and respond most gently -
My child, waste not your breath in cautioning me,
I am the spirit of Vyas that wrote krishna to life,
I am the law of Christ that parted the Red Sea.

I am in one, I am in all -
I am the universe in a brain.
I am creation, I am destruction,
After a long drought,
I am the monsoon rain.

I am not a person, the person is merely a vessel.
I am but expansion of the past giants,
I am the spirit supreme, I am but love universal.

I am the spirit of love,
you are the spirit of love,
spirit knows no separation.
Heart supreme is being supreme,
No heart is higher than
the one untainted by division.

Eyes see only what the heart knows to be true.
When the heart knows nothing but love,
wherever you look you find a loved one anew.

Animals don't look like animals these days,
some of them look quite fancy, suits and all.
But when you see family in every person you meet,
that's the first sign that you have become human.

Being of heart resists no hurt,
they savor poison like fine wine.
The benevolent takes no notice of betrayal,
while the somnolent just moan and whine.

Importune not the heart
with the fear of misfortune.
Heart is the origin of all fortune,
both of earth and of heaven.

Part 26

Heaven is here, right here on earth,
Heaven unfolds when you make someone smile.
Heaven is not a place somewhere up there,
Heaven is a moment, outside the animal exile.

Someone's smile is your heaven,
when you are the one to cause it.
Tears of joy are heaven,
when you are the reason behind it.

For each tear of suffering you wipe,
you lay the foundation of heaven.
For each mind you lift up without agenda,
you wipe out a bit of all living hell.

It is life that makes heaven and hell,
Life lived for others is heaven,
life selfish is purgatory.
Live so you could set an example of life,
and you'll find emancipation from all textual fantasy.

Grow out of the kindergarten of scripture,
Earn your admittance into the university of love.

Born by the Ganges,
Reborn by Bosphorus.
The name is Human,
Reformador of Earth.

Thus speaks the sapiens on guard,
Thus speaks the armor of the world.
Centipedes may mock your conviction,
Never apologize for your volcanic guts.

Creatures with second-hand spine
burn with envy at the sight of a daring backbone.
They cannot do much with their shallow life,
so they get some satisfaction
by mocking the cause of their salvation.

Yes, I am the salvation of my humankind,
Just as much as you are my salvation.
Every human who takes the world on their shoulder,
Becomes the entire humankind's servant solution.

Every sultan is servant,
every servant is sultan.
Insects may call it grandiosity,
I call it, life of a humanitarian.

Sacrifice is my illumination,
Servanthood is my sultanet.
People are the reason of my life,
I got too much electricity to sit and wait.

The wait is over, the moment
you realize your electricity.
All myths of second coming will fade away,
once you realize, all this time
you have been the holy trinity.

There is no trinity,
There is only unity -
Unity of human with the human -
All else is but make-believe divinity.

Abandon all make-believe,
that makes the mind lose the mind.
Stand up electrified and light up the world,
instead of living perpetually blind.

All sight is blind-sight,
that makes the being blind of its own strength.
Blame nobody, burden nobody,
just wake up a walking god - o reformer valiant.

Part 27

Valiance sleeps in your veins,
Volcano hides in your nerves.
Just once, strip your mind of all slavery,
And you'll be your liberty, not the nimrods.

Strip yourself of all slavery,
Rescue the world from the clutches of nimrods.
Nimrods only rule so long as the giants sleep,
Wake up, o giant - hate is breaking all records.

Who the hell are the nimrods to give you a break!
You are the break that this world needs.
They may need weapons and dollars to peddle hate,
All you need is a hateless heart,
that gives in to neither tradition nor greed.

Be the most awaited tear
upon the primal fabric of hate.
Rip that fabric to apart
with nothing but an unsubmissive conscience.

Submission to division
is the death of a human.
Human who submits to no inhumanity
is the walking torch of unification.

Unification is life,
Division is death.
Life unified is life divine,
Life divided is a cataclysmic disgrace.

No scripture has the authority
to define what is divine, what is not.
It is only a nonsectarian heart that reveals,
what is sacrilege, and what is not.

Kindness is grace,
hate is disgrace.
It is so simple, and yet,
bigots can't fathom simpleness.

Be the sample of simple love,
not a mockery of everything civilized.
Cut every last tie with sectarianism,
leave the uncivilization to the uncivilized.

BIBLIOGRAPHY

162

Archer M., (2000), Being Human: The Problem of Agency. Cambridge University Press.

Adolphs R (2003) Cognitive neuroscience of human social behaviour. Nature Rev Neurosci 4: 165–178.

Adolphs R, Tranel D, Damasio AR (2003) Dissociable neural systems for recognizing emotions. Brain Cogn 52: 61–69.

Andresen, Jensine, and Robert Forman, eds. Cognitive Models and Spiritual Maps. Bowling Green, Ohio: Imprint Academic, 2000.

Bernstein R.J., (1971), Praxis and Action: Contemporary Philosophies of Human Activity. Philadelphia: University of Pennsylvania Press.

Bernstein R.J., (1976), The Restructuring Social and Political Thought.

Bogen, J.E.(1995a), 'On the neurophysiology of consciousness: Part I. An overview', Consciousness and Cognition, 4.

Bogen, J.E. (1995b), 'On the neurophysiology of consciousness: Part II. Constraining the semantic problem', Consciousness and Cognition, 4.

Bremner, J. D., R. Soufer, et al. (2001). "Gender differences in cognitive and neural correlates of remembrance of emotional words." Psychopharmacol Bull 35 (3).

Brothers, L. (2002). The social brain: A project for integrating primate behavior and neurophysiology in a new domain. In J. T. Cacioppo et al. (Eds.), Foundations in neuroscience. Cambridge, MA: MIT Press.

Buss, D. D. (2003). Evolutionary Psychology: The New Science of Mind, 2nd ed. New York: Allyn & Bacon.

Buss, D. M. (1989). "Conflict between the sexes: Strategic interference and the evocation of anger and upset." J Pers Soc Psychol 56 (5).

Buss, D. M. (1995). "Psychological sex differences. Origins through sexual selection." Am Psychol 50 (3).

Buss, D. M., and D. P. Schmitt (1993). "Sexual strategies theory: An evolutionary perspective on human mating." Psychol Rev 100 (2).

Chomsky Noam, (2016) Who Rules the World?

Churchland, P.S. (1986), Neurophilosophy (Cambridge, MA: The MIT Press).

Churchland, P.S. & Ramachandran, V.S. (1993), 'Filling in: Why Dennett is wrong', in Dennett and His Critics:

Demystifying Mind, ed. B. Dahlbom (Oxford: Blackwell Scientific Press).

Churchland, P.S., Ramachandran, V.S. & Sejnowski, T.J. (1994), 'A critique of pure vision', in Large- scale Neuronal Theories of the Brain, ed. C. Koch & J.L. Davis (Cambridge, MA: The MIT Press).

Crick, F. (1994), The Astonishing Hypothesis: The Scientific Search for the Soul (New York: Simon and Schuster).

Crick, F. (1996), 'Visual perception: rivalry and consciousness', Nature, 379.

Crick, F. & Koch, C. (1992), 'The problem of consciousness', Scientific American, 267.

d'Aquili, Eugene. "Senses of Reality in Science and Religion." Zygon 17, no 4 (1982)

d'Aquili, Eugene. "The Biopsychological Determinants of Religious Ritual Behavior." Zygon 10, no. 1 (1975)

d'Aquili, Eugene. "The Myth-Ritual Complex: A Biogenetic Structural Analysis." Zygon 18, no. 3 (1983)

d'Aquili, Eugene, and Andrew Newberg. The Mystical Mind: Probing the Biology of Religious Experience. Minneapolis: Fortress Press, 1999.

Damasio, A. (1994) Descartes' Error: Emotion, Reason and the Human Brain. New York, Putnams.

Damasio, A. (1999) The Feeling of What Happens: Body, Emotion and the Making of Consciousness. London, Heinemann.

Darwin, C. (1859) On the Origin of Species by Means of Natural Selection. London, Murray.

Darwin, C. (1871) The Descent of Man and Selection in Relation to Sex. London, John Murray.

Dawkins, R. (1976) The Selfish Gene. Oxford, Oxford University Press; a new edition, with additional material, was published in 1989.

Dewhurst, Kenneth, and A. W. Beard. "Sudden Religious Conversions in Temporal Lobe Epilepsy." British Journal of Psychiatry 117 (1970)

Dewhurst K, Beard AW. Sudden religious conversions in temporal lobe epilepsy. 1970 Epilepsy Behav 2003

Devinsky O, Lai G. Spirituality and religion in epilepsy. Epilepsy Behav 2008.

E. Horvitz, "One Hundred Year Study on Artificial Intelligence: Reflections and Framing," ed: Stanford University, 2014.

Eckhart Meister, Selected Writings

Farah, M.J. (1989), 'The neural basis of mental imagery', Trends in Neurosciences, 10.

Freud, S. "Selected papers on hysteria and other psychoneuroses" Journal of Nervous and Mental Disease 1909.

Freud, S. "The Origin and Development of Psychoanalysis", 1910

Freud, S. "Psychopathology of everyday life", 1914

Freud, S. "Beyond the Pleasure Principle", 1920

Frith, C.D. & Dolan, R.J. (1997), 'Abnormal beliefs: Delusions and memory', Paper presented at the May, 1997, Harvard Conference on Memory and Belief.

Gay, Volney, ed. Neuroscience and Religion. Plymouth, UK: Lexington Books, 2009.

Gazzaniga, M. S. (1985). The social brain. New York: Basic Books.

Gazzaniga, M.S. (1993), 'Brain mechanisms and conscious experience', Ciba Foundation Symposium, 174.

Geschwind N. "Behavioural changes in temporal lobe epilepsy". Psychol Med. 1979.

Gellhorn, E., Kiely, W.F. "Mystical states of consciousness: neurophysiological and clinical aspects." J Nerv Ment Dis. 1972;154:399-405.

Gilbert SL, Dobyns WB, Lahn BT (2005) Genetic links between brain development and brain evolution. Nat Rev Genet 6.

Gray JA. The Psychology of Fear and Stress. 2nd ed. New York, NY: Cambridge University Press; 1988.

Gloor, P. (1992), 'Amygdala and temporal lobe epilepsy', in The Amygdala: Neurobiological Aspects of Emotion, Memory and Mental

Dysfunction, ed J.P. Aggleton (New York: Wiley-Liss).

Gross CG, Rocha-Miranda CE, Bender DB (1972) Visual properties of neurons in the inferotemporal cortex of the macaque. J Neurophysiol 35: 96–111.

Guevara Che, The Motorcycle Diaries, 1992

Hardy, G. H. (1940). Ramanujan. Cambridge: Cambridge University Press.

Hall, Daniel, Keith Meador, and Harold Koenig. "Measuring Religiousness in Health Research: Review and Critique." Journal of Religion and Health 47, no. 2 (2008)

Harris, Sam, Jonas Kaplan, Ashley Curiel, Susan Bookheimer, Marco Iacoboni, and Mark Cohen. "The Neural Correlates of Religious and Nonreligious Belief." PLoS One 4, no. 10 (October 1, 2009)

Halgren, E. (1992), 'Emotional neurophysiology of the amygdala within the context of human cognition', in The Amygdala: Neurobiological Aspects of Emotion, Memory and Mental Dysfunction, ed J.P. Aggleton (New York: Wiley-Liss).

Halligan PW, Fink GR, Marshal JC, Vallar G. 2003. Spatial cognition: evidence from visual neglect. Trends Cogn Sci.

Handbook of Emotions, Edited by Michael Lewis, Jeannette M. Haviland-Jones, and Lisa Feldman Barrett, The Guilford Press; 3rd edition (2010).

Hameroff, S.R. and Penrose, R. (1996) Conscious events as orchestrated space-time selections. Journal of Consciousness Studies 3(1), 36-53; also reprinted in J. Shear (ed.) (1997) Explaining Consciousness-The Hard Problem. Cambridge, MA, MIT Press, 177-95.

Harding, D.E. (1961) On Having no Head: Zen and the Re-Discovery of the Obvious. London, Buddhist Society.

Hardy, A. (1979) The Spiritual Nature of Man: A Study of Contemporary Religious Experience. Oxford, Clarendon Press.

Harre, R. and Gillett, G. (1994) The Discursive Mind. Thousand Oaks, CA, Sage.

Haugeland, J. (ed.) (1997) Mind Design II: Philosophy, Psychology, Artificial Intelligence. Cambridge, MA, MIT Press.

Hauser, M.D. (2000) Wild Minds: What Animals Really Think. New York, Henry Holt and Co.; London, Penguin.

Hilgard, E.R. (1986) Divided Consciousness: Multiple Controls in Human Thought and Action. New York, Wiley.

Hilton, E.N., Lundberg, T.R. Transgender Women in the Female Category of Sport: Perspectives on Testosterone Suppression and Performance Advantage. Sports Med 51, 199–214 (2021).

Hitler, Adolf. Mein Kampf, 1925

Hodgson, R. (1891) A case of double consciousness. Proceedings of the Society for Psychical Research 7, 221-58.

Hofstadter, D.R. and Dennett, D.C. (eds) (1981) The Mind's I: Fantasies and Reflections on Self and Soul. London, Penguin.

Holland, J. (ed.) (2001) Ecstasy: The Complete Guide: A Comprehensive Look at the Risks and Benefits of MDMA. Rochester, VT, Park Street Press.

Holmes, D.S. (1987) The influence of meditation versus rest on physiological arousal. In M. West (ed.)

The Psychology of Meditation. Oxford, Clarendon Press, 81-103.

Holmstrom, David. 1992, Christian Science Monitor

Holloway RL (1996) Evolution of the human brain. In: Lock A, Peters CR (eds) Handbook of human symbolic evolution. Oxford University Press, Oxford

Jeannerod M (1988) The neural and behavioural organization of goal-directed movements. Clarendon Press, Oxford.

Johnson-Frey SH, Maloof FR, Newman-Norlund R, Farrer C, Inati S, Grafton ST (2003) Actions or hand-objects interactions? Human inferior frontal cortex and action observation. Neuron 39: 1053–1058.

Jackson, F. (1982) Epiphenomenal qualia. Philosophical Quarterly 32, 127-36.

James, W. (1890) The Principles of Psychology (2 volumes). London, Macmillan.

James, W. (1902) The Varieties of Religious Experience: A Study in Human Nature. New York and London, Longmans, Green and Co.

Jansen, K. (2001) Ketamine: Dreams and Realities. Sarasota, FL, Multidisciplinary Association for Psychedelic Studies.

Jay, M. (ed.) (1999) Artificial Paradises: A Drugs Reader. London, Penguin.

Jaynes, J. (1976) The Origin of Consciousness in the Breakdown of the Bicameral Mind. New York, Houghton Mifflin.

Kandel, E. R. In Search of Memory: The Emergence of a New Science of Mind, W. W. Norton & Company (2007).

Kandel E. R. Schwartz JH, Jessel TM. Principles of neural sciences. New York; McGraw Hill, 2000.

Kanwisher, N. (2001) Neural events and perceptual awareness. Cognition 79, 89-113; also reprinted inS. Dehaene (ed.) The Cognitive Neuroscience of Consciousness. Cambridge, MA, MIT Press, 89-113.

Kihlstrom, J.F. (1996) Perception without awareness of what is perceived, learning without awareness of what is learned. In M. Velmans (ed.) The Science of Consciousness. London, Routledge, 23-46.

Kosslyn, S.M. (1980) Image and Mind. Cambridge, MA, Harvard University Press.

Kosslyn, S.M. (1988) Aspects of a cognitive neuroscience of mental imagery. Science 240, 1621-6.

Kjaer, Troels, Camilla Bertelsen, Paola Piccini, David Brooks, Jorgen Alving, and Hans Lou. "Increased Dopamine Tone during Meditation- Induced Change of Consciousness." Cognitive Brain Research 13, no. 2 (April 2002)

Kölmel HW. 1985. Complex visual hallucinations in the hemianopic field. J Neurol Neurosurg Psychiatry.

Koenig, Harold. "Research on Religion, Spirituality, and Mental Health: A Review." Canadian Journal of Psychiatry 54, no. 5 (May 2009)

Koenig, Harold, ed. Handbook of Religion and Mental Health. San Diego, CA: Academic Press, 1998

Kraepelin E. Psychiatry: A Textbook for Students and Physicians. New York, NY: Science History Publications; 1990.

Lauglin, Charles, John McManus, and Eugene d'Aquili. Brain, Symbol, and Experience. 2nd ed. New York: Columbia University Press, 1992

Lakoff, G. and M. Johnson (1999). Philosophy in the flesh. Basic Books: New York.

LeDoux, J. E. (1996). The emotional brain. New York: Simon & Schuster.

LeDoux, J.E. (1992), 'Emotion and the amygdala', in The Amygdala: Neurobiological Aspects of Emo- tion, Memory and Mental Dysfunction, ed J.P. Aggleton (New York: Wiley-Liss).

Levin, D.T. and Simons, D.J. (1997) Failure to detect changes to attended objects in motion pictures. Psychonomic Bulletin and Review 4, 501-6.

Levine,J. (1983) Materialism and qualia: the explanatory gap. Pacific Philosophical Quarterly 64, 354-61.

Levine,J. (2001) Purple Haze: The Puzzle of Consciousness. New York, Oxford University Press. Levine, S. (1979) A Gradual Awakening. New York, Doubleday.

Levinson, B.W. (1965) States of awareness during general anaesthesia. British Journal of Anaesthesia 37, 544-6.

Lewicki, P., Czyzewska, M. and Hoffman, H. (1987) Unconscious acquisition of complex procedural knowledge. Journal of Experimental Psychology: Learning, Memory and Cognition 13, 523-30.

Naskar, Abhijit. "What is Mind?", 2016

Naskar, Abhijit. "Love, God & Neurons: Memoir of A Scientist who found himself by getting lost", 2016

Naskar, Abhijit. "Principia Humanitas", 2017

Naskar, Abhijit. "We Are All Black: A Treatise on Racism", 2017

Naskar, Abhijit. "Either Civilized or Phobic: A Treatise on Homosexuality", 2017

Naskar, Abhijit. "Build Bridges not Walls: In the name of Americana", 2018

Naskar, Abhijit. "Citizens of Peace: Beyond the Savagery of Sovereignty", 2019

Naskar, Abhijit. "The Constitution of The United Peoples of Earth", 2019

Naskar, Abhijit. "Mission Reality", 2019

Naskar, Abhijit. "Good Scientist: When Science and Service Combine", 2020

Newberg, Andrew, and Jeremy Iversen. "The Neural Basis of the Complex Mental Task of Meditation: Neurotransmitter and Neurochemical Considerations." Medical Hypotheses 61, no. 2 (2003).

Newberg, Andrew. "How God Changes Your Brain: An Introduction to Jewish Neurotheology", CCAR

Journal: The Reform Jewish Quarterly, Winter 2016.

Newberg, Andrew, and Stephanie Newberg. "A Neuropsychological Perspective on Spiritual Development." In Handbook of Spiritual Development in Childhood and Adolescence, edited by Eugene Roehlkepartain, Pamela King, Linda Wagener, and Peter Benson. London: Sage Publications, Inc., 2005

Newberg, Andrew. "The Neurotheology Link An Intersection Between Spirituality and Health", Alternative and Complimentary Therapies, Vol 21 No 1, February 2015.

Newberg, Andrew, Nancy Wintering, Dharma Khalsa, Hannah Roggenkamp, and Mark Waldman. "Meditation Effects on Cognitive Function and Cerebral Blood Flow in Subjects with Memory Loss: A Preliminary Study." Journal of Alzheimer's Disease 20, no. 2 (2010)

Nash, M. (1995), 'Glimpses of the mind', Time.

Nesse RM. Proximate and evolutionary studies of anxiety, stress and depression: synergy at the interface. Neurosci Biobehav Rev. 1999;23:895-903.

Nicolelis, Miguel. (2011) "Beyond Boundaries: The New Neuroscience of Connecting Brains with Machines---and How It Will Change Our Lives", Times Books

O'Hara, K. and Scutt, T. (1996) There is no hard problem of consciousness. Journal of Consciousness Studies 3(4), 290-302, reprinted in J. Shear (ed.) (1997) Explaining Consciousness. Cambridge, MA, MIT Press, 69-82.

O'Regan, J.K. and Noe, A. (2001) A sensorimotor account of vision and visual consciousness. Behavioral and Brain Sciences 24(5), 883-917.

Ornstein, R.E. (1977) The Psychology of Consciousness (2nd edn). New York, Harcourt.

Ornstein, R.E. (1986) The Psychology of Consciousness (3rd edn). New York, Pehguin.

Ornstein, R.E. (1992) The Evolution of Consciousness. New York, Touchstone.

Penfield W, Faulk ME (1955) The insula: further observations on its function. Brain 78: 445– 470.

Penrose, R. (1994), Shadows of the Mind (Oxford: Oxford University Press).

Penrose, R. (1989), The Emperor's New Mind: Concerning Computers, Minds and The Laws of Physics (Oxford: Oxford University Press).

Persinger, "'I would kill in God's name' role of sex, weekly church attendance, report of a religious experience and limbic lability" Perceptual and Motor Skills 1997.

Persinger "Experimental simulation of the God experience" Neurotheology 2003.

Persinger, Corradini, Clement, Keaney, et al "Neurotheology and its convergence with neuroquantology" NeuroQuantology 2010.

Persinger. "The neuropsychiatry of paranormal experiences". J Neuropsychiatry Clin Neurosci 2001.

Persinger. "Neuropsychological bases of god beliefs", New York: Praeger, 1987

Persinger. "Temporal lobe epileptic signs and correlative behaviors displayed by normal populations", Journal of General Psychology, 1986

Perry BD, Pollard R. Homeostasis, stress, trauma, and adaptation. A neurodevelopmental view of childhood trauma. Child Adolesc Psychiatr Clin N Am. 1998;7:33.

Ramachandran VS. Behavioral and magnetoencephalographic correlates of plasticity in the adult human brain. Proc Natl Acad Sci USA 1993; 90: 10413–20.

Ramachandran VS. Plasticity and functional recovery in neurology. Clin Med 2005; 5: 368–73.

Rock I, Victor J. Vision and touch: an experimentally created conflict between the two senses. Science 1964; 143: 594–6.

Roberts, TA; Smalley, J; Ahrendt, D (December 2020). "Effect of gender affirming hormones on athletic performance in transwomen and transmen: implications for sporting organisations and legislators". British Journal of Sports Medicine. 55 (11): 577–583

Royet JP, Plailly J, Delon-Martin C, Kareken DA, Segebarth C (2003) fMRI of emotional responses to odors: influence of hedonic valence and judgment, handedness, and gender. Neuroimage 20: 713–728.

Rozin R Haidt J and McCauley CR (2000) Disgust. In: Lewis M, Haviland-Jones JM (eds) Handbook of Emotion. 2nd Edition. Guilford Press, New York, pp 637–653.

Saxe R, Carey S, Kanwisher N (2004) Understanding other minds: linking developmental psychology and functional neuroimaging. Annu Rev Psychol 55: 87–124.

S. J. Russell and P. Norvig, Artificial intelligence: a modern approach (3rd edition): Prentice Hall, 2009.

Singer T, Seymour B, O'Doherty J, Kaube H, Dolan RJ, Frith CD (2004) Empathy for pain involves the affective but not the sensory components of pain. Science 303: 1157–1162.

Smith A (1759) The theory of moral sentiments (ed. 1976). Clarendon Press, Oxford.

Schilling, Vincent. 2017, indian country today

Stein, Stephen K. 2017, The Sea in World History: Exploration, Travel, and Trade

Tesla N. "My Inventions", 1919

T. R. Society, "Machine learning: the power and promise of computers that learn by example," ed. The Royal Society, 2017.

Tomasello M, Call J (1997) Primate cognition. Oxford University Press, Oxford